OTHER BOOKS BY HELEN EXLEY:

Over 50s' Jokes   Cat Jokes
Over 60s' Jokes   365 Happy Days!
Over 70s' Jokes   The gift of Happiness
Golf Jokes   Senior Moments 365

EDITED BY HELEN EXLEY

Published in 2019 by Helen Exley®LONDON in Great Britain.
Design, selection and arrangement © Helen Exley Creative Ltd 2019.
All the words by Stuart & Linda Macfarlane, Odile Dormeuil, Brian
Clyde, Pam Brown, Amanda Bell, Linda Gibson, Helen Exley,
Charlotte Gray, Mathilde & Sébastien Forestier, Bill Stott, Pamela
Dugdale, Peter Gray and Helen Thomson are copyright © Helen
Exley Creative Ltd 2019.
Cartoons copyright © Bill Stott 2019.
The moral rights of the authors have been asserted.

12 11 10 9 8 7 6 5 4 3 2 1

ISBN: 978-1-78485-242-9

Helen Exley® LONDON,
16 Chalk Hill, Watford, Herts WD19 4BG, UK
www.helenexley.com

Over 80's Jokes

CARTOONS BY BILL STOTT

Helen Exley

The best tunes are played on the oldest fiddles.

SIGMUND ENGEL

The photographer had just taken a picture of a man on his ninety-ninth birthday. He thanked the old gentleman, saying, "I hope I'll be around to take your picture when you're a hundred." The old man replied, "Why not? You look pretty healthy."

AUTHOR UNKNOWN

The hair
may go.
The teeth
may go.
The memory
may go.
But the folly
goes on forever.

STUART & LINDA MACFARLANE

Youth, large, lusty, loving –
Youth, full of grace,
force, fascination!
Do you know that Old Age
may come after you
with equal grace, force,
fascination?

WALT WHITMAN

Old age is when it takes you
longer to get over a good time
than to have it.

E. C. MCKENZIE

Life is like a bottle of Champagne:
full of fizz, razzmatazz and
celebration. It's rather sad that,
when you are so old,
you become incapable of getting
the cork out.

STUART & LINDA MACFARLANE

The old can go on exciting trips,
just like the young.
Trouble is they are asleep most
of the time.

ODILE DORMEUIL

Be positive today for tomorrow is going to be worse.

BRIAN CLYDE

How one loves a deep, warm,
bubbly bath – a pleasure
only overshadowed by the question
of how one is going to get out.

PAM BROWN

An old married couple
were lying in bed and the wife
said wistfully,
"Do you remember, when we were
first married and got into bed,
you hardly gave me time
to get my stockings off."
"Ah," sighed the old man,
"now you'd have time to knit
yourself a pair."

AUTHOR UNKNOWN

A woman walked up to a little old man rocking in a chair on his porch.

"I couldn't help noticing how happy you look," she said. "What's your secret for a long, happy life?"

"I smoke three packets of cigarettes a day," he said. "I also drink a case of whiskey a week, eat fatty foods, and never exercise."

"That's amazing," the woman said. "How old are you?"

"Twenty six," he said.

JOE CLARO

I took a trip down memory lane and got totally lost.

STUART & LINDA MACFARLANE

Six months ago my husband
started running ten miles
every single day.
I just hope that at some point
he remembers to turn back.

AMANDA BELL

Eat vitamin pills,
exercise regularly,
and remember
to put your
dentures back in.

HELEN EXLEY

At 82 I'm not as strong
as I was when I was 22,
I am not as fit
as I was when I was 22
and I'm definitely
not as good looking
as I was when I was 22.
But I have one characteristic
that all the 80 year old ladies adore –
I've forgotten...

Dear Diary:

This has been a wonderful day.

I didn't get lost once.

I didn't have the embarrassment of
meeting someone whose name
I couldn't remember.

I didn't buy courgettes instead of milk
at the supermarket.

Yes – I have had a great day
sitting with my feet up watching
box sets on the television.

STUART & LINDA MACFARLANE

Oh, to be Spanish, and be encouraged to dance flamenco when one is ninety-five.

PAM BROWN

You can't turn
back the clock.
But you can wind
it up again.

BONNIE PRUDDEN

A Missouri husband said sadly,
"It's terrible to grow old alone.
My wife hasn't had a birthday
for many years."

E. C. MCKENZIE

At age eighty-two,
I sometimes feel like a twenty-year-old,
but there's seldom one around.

MILTON BERLE

Never retire! Do what you do and
keep doing it. But don't do it on Friday.
Take Friday off. Friday, Saturday,
and Sunday, do sexual activities,
watch movies. Then from Monday
to Thursday, do what you've been
doing all your life, unless it's lifting
bags of potatoes off the back of a truck.
I mean, after eighty-five that's hard to do.

MEL BROOKS

EXCUSES

I'd love to go out with you but my hair
is at the dry cleaners.
I never date a person who wears
second-hand dentures.
I never date anyone who's more
than 50% synthetic parts.
Sorry, I'm planning a complete clean
and polish of my dentures that night.
Go out with you?
My head says yes but my pacemaker
says no!

MATHILDE & SÉBASTIEN FORESTIER

Eighty-Eight and still all our own teeth... Mostly rotten.

BILL STOTT

You're never too old to become younger.

MAE WEST

You are never too young
to fall in love and never too old
to wish you had.

KERI NOBLE

At night I unzip this skin
and hang it on a chair.
At night I walk free, and easily.
Take old familiar paths.
Greet old familiar friends...
Sad that morning comes
and I must climb into
that ageing skin again.
But it's been a lovely break.

PAM BROWN

If the young knew!

Life is like a rich fruit cake.
When you're young you guzzle it
with passion.
When you're old you
nibble it slowly – you know it
will give you indigestion.

MATHILDE & SÉBASTIEN FORESTIER

It's not perfect, but to me
on balance Right Now is a lot better
than the Good Old Days.

MAEVE BINCHY

– if the old could!

ALOIS VERRE

If you want a thing well done,
get a couple of old broads to do it.

BETTE DAVIS

Her face looks as if it had worn out two bodies.

NEW ENGLAND SAYING

When one is old one becomes flushed with pride when the chiropodist says one has good feet.

PAM BROWN

There are three ways to tell
if you're getting on:
people of your own age start
looking older than you;
you become convinced you're
suddenly equipped with
a snooze button;
and you get symptoms
in the places you used to get urges.

DENIS NORDEN

As we grow older,
our bodies get shorter
and our anecdotes longer.

ROBERT QUILLEN

I still have two abiding passions.
One is my model railway,
the other – women.
But at the age of eighty-nine,
I find I am getting just a little too old
for model railways.

PIERRE MONTEUX

Being over eighty is when
the dreams you had at
twenty have to be overhauled…
to allow for your back,
your feet and your leaks.

PAM BROWN

My idea of exercise is a good brisk sit down.

PHYLLIS DILLER

YOU'RE GETTING ON WHEN
...you navigate by toilets.
...you're on first name terms
with your doctor, optician, chiropodist,
dietician, and beautician.
...you keep a timetable
for taking your daily pills.
...your clothes are back in fashion.
...you introduce a colleague
to your wife and can't remember
your wife's name.
...a visit to the beautician
lasts eight hours.

LINDA GIBSON

I exercise
every morning
without fail.
Up, down!
Up, down!
And then
the other eyelid.

ANTHONY HOPKINS

Eighty years old!
No eyes left, no ears, no teeth,
no legs, no wind!
And when all is said and done,
how astonishingly well
one does without them!

PAUL CLAUDEL

An archaeologist is the best
husband a woman can have;
the older she gets,
the more interested he is in her.

AGATHA CHRISTIE

Old is...
when you look
in the mirror
and think to yourself
"Aren't I wise."

MARCELLA MARKHAM

Gray sideburns make some men
look distinguished. On me
it just looks like I ran out of dye.

ROBERT ORBEN

By the time most folks learn to behave themselves they're too old to do anything else.

E. C. MCKENZIE

The only thing I regret about my past is the length of it.

TALLULAH BANKHEAD

When you get older you just naturally slow up. Your body doesn't work as well; you wear out a little. I'm waiting for this to happen to me. And when it does I'll make the best of it. Right now I'm 100, and there isn't a thing I can do now that I couldn't do when I was 18. I can do more now than when I was 18... I did nothing when I was 18... I was pathetic when I was 18... I was even worse when I was 17... I wasn't so hot when I was 25, either. I saved everything for now. I hate to brag, but I'm very good at now.

GEORGE BURNS

What's the good of having
something to look forward to,
if I can't remember what it was?

ASHLEIGH BRILLIANT

French newspaper reporters
asked philosopher Fontanelle
to name the great love of his life.
"I can't tell you yet,"
said Fontanelle,
"I am only ninety-five."

AUTHOR UNKNOWN

The four stages
in accepting old age;
denial,
anger,
despair,
having a
bloody good time.

STUART & LINDA MACFARLANE

I've found the secret
of my eternal youth.
I lie about my age!

BOB HOPE

Age is irrelevant,
unless, of course, you happen
to be a bottle of wine.

JOAN COLLINS

There are three signs of old age;
hearing fading, loss of memory and…
there are three signs of old age;
hearing fading, loss of memory and…

LINDA GIBSON

At eighty I believe I am a far
more cheerful person than I was
at twenty or thirty. I most definitely
would not want to be a teenager again.
Youth may be glorious but it is
also painful to endure.
Moreover, what is called youth
is not youth; it is rather something
like premature old age.

HENRY MILLER

If you live to be one hundred,
you've got it made.
Very few people die past that age.

GEORGE BURNS

Old age is when you

nap between sleeps.

MATHILDE & SÉBASTIEN FORESTIER

"What's the matter little boy,"
said the old codger when he saw
the lad sitting on the kerb crying.
"I'm crying because I can't do
what the big boys do," he said.
The old man sat on the kerb
and started crying too.

GEORGE COOTE

It's funny how
we never get too old
to learn some new
ways to be foolish.

E. C. MCKENZIE

'Tis a maxim with me to be young
as long as one can:
there is nothing can pay one for that
invaluable ignorance which is
the companion of youth;
those sanguine groundless hopes,
and that lively vanity, which make
all the happiness of life.
To my extreme mortification
I grow wiser every day.

LADY MARY WORTLEY MONTAGU

Just think, if only you could
snap your fingers on the birthday
you wanted and never grow older!
HUH! Birthdays
won't even let you do that because
you've got that much arthritis
your fingers won't snap.

SUSAN CURZON

...one advantage of age
is it gives you license to act eccentric
or be moody and get away with it.

BETTE DAVIS

You are only young once,
but you can be immature
for a lifetime.

JOHN P. GRIER

Getting older has some benefits...
Call it a "Senior Moment"
and you can get away with pretty
much anything.

AUTHOR UNKNOWN

Life is one long wild party – but the morning after is horrendous.

MATHILDE & SÉBASTIEN FORESTIER

Why Not?

A reporter was interviewing a man
who was believed to be the oldest
resident in town.

"May I ask how old you are?"
the newsman inquired.

"I just turned a hundred this week,"
the oldster proudly replied.

"Great! Do you suppose you'll see
another hundred?" the reporter asked
playfully. "Well," said the man
thoughtfully, "I'm stronger now
than when I started the first
one hundred!"

AUTHOR UNKNOWN

How is it that our memory
is good enough to retain the least
triviality that happens to us,
and yet not good enough
to recollect how often we have told
it to the same person?

FRANÇOIS DE LA ROCHEFOUCAULD

I pray that I
may seem,
though I die old,
a foolish,
passionate man.

WILLIAM BUTLER YEATS

Darling, when you are young,
never smile. It causes wrinkles.
When you are old,
smile all the time. It hides them.

MARLENE DIETRICH

With age comes skills.
It's called multi-tasking.
I can laugh, cough,
sneeze, and pee
all at the same time.

Old age is a

shipwreck.

CHARLES DE GAULLE

If you're odd enough and old enough people will stop thinking of you as peculiar and regard you as an interesting eccentric.

PAMELA DUGDALE

So how do you know
when you've become an oldie?
You know you are an oldie if you:

• Think your spouse looks great
with white hair.
• Are amazed to learn that the golden
oldies radio station plays modern music
from the sixties instead of oldies music
from the forties.
• Remember when Frank Sinatra had hair.
• Remember Frank Sinatra.
• Have pictures in your photo album
of people you don't recognise.

NIELA ELIASON

Geriatric Chat-Up Line

•You have a beautiful smile –
I bet you look even better
with your dentures in.

STUART & LINDA MACFARLANE

Janice:
"My husband tricked me
into marrying him.
Before we married he said he was
a multi-millionaire."
Bernice:
"He is a multi-millionaire, isn't he?"
Janice:
"Yes. But he also said he was eighty-one
and in poor health –
but I've just found out he's only
eighty and in perfect condition."

KEVIN GOLDSTEIN-JACKSON

Every day above the ground is a good one!

FRANK JANSEN

Oh, to be seventy again!

GEORGES CLEMENCEAU

Friends like to do the same things
together as they did when they
were young.
Only more slowly.

ODILE DORMEUIL

I bought that electric comb
with the little light on it.
With my hair, the problem isn't
combing it. It's finding it.

ROBERT ORBEN

At eighty you can embarrass
youngsters by smothering them
in soppy kisses.
Instead of taking your grandchildren
on outings, they take you.
You no longer get zits.
You get to ride at top speed in ambulances.
You can pretend that you don't hear
what people are saying.

MATHILDE & SÉBASTIEN FORESTIER

Every morning
I get up,
I read the obits page.
If my name's
not there, I shave.

GEORGE BURNS

Decrepit?
I have the stamina
of an ox,
the sex drive
of a bull and
the body of
a pink, psychedelic
elephant!

MATHILDE & SÉBASTIEN FORESTIER

I would say
I was ninety-nine,
dahling.

ZSA ZSA GABOR

You're never too old

You know you're getting older
when you can't get
your rocking chair started.

AUTHOR UNKNOWN

to do goofy stuff.

WARD CLEAVER

Old age is when most of the names
in your little black book are doctors.

E. C. MCKENZIE

By the time you're 80 years old
you've learnt everything.
You only have to remember it.

GEORGE BURNS

Old age is when you go on
a protest march
because you need the exercise.

AUTHOR UNKNOWN

One advantage of
getting old.
So many people do not
share my past that
I am free to invent it.

ALFRED KAZIN

…the products you bought
with lifetime guarantees were
made by companies that have
since gone out of business.

MARTIN A RAGAWAY

I wish I had started out
at the age of ninety-six.
Look how much fun
I would have had!

EUBIE BLAKE

I prefer to forget both pairs
of glasses and pass my
declining years saluting strange
women and grandfather clocks.

OGDEN NASH

You know you're getting old
when you stoop to tie
your shoes and wonder
what else you can do while
you're down there.

GEORGE BURNS

One of the nice things
about old age
is that you can whistle
while you brush your teeth.

E. C. MCKENZIE

Another benefit of
great maturity is that you're worth
a fortune. You have silver in
your hair, gold in your teeth,
stones in your kidneys,
lead in your feet, mineral deposits
in your joints, and natural gas
in your stomach.

JASON LOVE

I don't feel old,
in fact,
I don't feel
anything till noon.
Then it's time
for my nap.

BOB HOPE

There are three periods in life:
youth,
middle age and
"How well you look."

NELSON A. ROCKEFELLER

Old ladies have one
last chance at defiance –
pink or blue or violet hair.

PAM BROWN

After the age of eighty,
all contemporaries are friends.

MADAME DE DINO

Nostalgia isn't what

it used to be. <small>SIMONE SIGNORET</small>

I get all my exercise acting
as a pallbearer to my friends
who exercise.

CHAUNCEY DEPEW

You can live
to be a hundred
if you give up
all the things
that make you
want to live
to be a hundred.

WOODY ALLEN

I don't know what the big deal is
about old age.
Old people who shine from inside
look ten to twenty years younger.

DOLLY PARTON

Everyone else
grows old
– but we stay comfortably
middle-aged.

ODILE DORMEUIL

If things get better
with age,
then I'm approaching
magnificent.

NICOLE BEALE

When I was fourteen,
I was the oldest I ever was.
I've been getting younger
ever since.

SHIRLEY TEMPLE

I have just calculated
that I have been alive
for 2,907,521,027 seconds.
Sadly I have wasted
14,211 of those seconds
doing the calculation.

STUART MACFARLANE

My ability to do algebra, trigonometry
and calculus hasn't changed at all
over the decades.
In my declining years they are still
the mystery they were when
I was a teenager.

AMANDA BELL

I have always felt that a woman
has the right to treat
the subject of her age
with ambiguity until, perhaps,
she passes into the realm
of over ninety.
Then it is better
she be candid with herself
and with the world.

HELENA RUBINSTEIN

At my age I'm envious of a stiff wind.

RODNEY DANGERFIELD

Life is for the old to enjoy and the young to look forward to.

AUTHOR UNKNOWN

Old age is when
you demonstrate a sporting skill.
And your back goes.

PETER GRAY

When you are eighty
youngsters give you their
seat on the bus –
if you give them a gentle prod
with your walking stick.

MATHILDE & SÉBASTIEN FORESTIER

Visiting choral groups depend
a great deal on the fact
that their ancient audience
cannot run away.

PAM BROWN

Y‍ou know you've had one birthday
too many when your cake
collapses from the weight
of the candles.

AUTHOR UNKNOWN

Old age is no place

Over eighty is when
you regret that you resisted
all those temptations.

RICHARD LEDERER

for sissies. BETTE DAVIS

Say I woke up
and I could read easily?
And my knees didn't creak?
For sure,
I'd know I was dead.

HELEN THOMSON

A distinguished French politician having celebrated his 90th birthday was asked by a friend:
"How do you find life now you are 90?"
"Fine when you consider the alternative."

SIR JOHN CORDINGLEY

After the effort
of getting out of bed
you need another nap.
You wake with that
"morning after" feeling
when you haven't done anything
the night before.
You forget that you're
absent minded.
You get out of breath
playing chess.

LINDA GIBSON

My friends and I still love
to play Scrabble even though
we are now all over eighty. We haven't
lost our touch and can come up with
some very interesting words.
I wish I could remember one!

BRIAN CLYDE

At my age,
when a girl flirts
with me in the movies,
she's after
my popcorn.

MILTON BERLE

At this age, being able
to remember something
is as good as an orgasm.

GLORIA STEINEM

You know your memory
has started to go when…
…you tear down the garden shed
you're in the middle of building.
…you have *déjà vu* about events
that happened five minutes ago.
…you find your keys but lose the house.
…you turn up late
for a dental appointment –
and you're the dentist.

MATHILDE & SÉBASTIEN FORESTIER

So many candles,

so little cake!

AUTHOR UNKNOWN

You know you're getting old when
the candles cost more than the cake.

BOB HOPE

THE TEETH
OF WISDOM
MAY WELL
BE FALSE.

ELLIOTT PRIEST

Like a prune,
you are not getting any better looking,
but you are getting sweeter.

N. D. STICE

If you live long enough,
the venerability factor creeps in;
you get accused of things
you never did
and praised for virtues
you never had.

I.F. STONE

Why is it that when
you get very, very old...
you think it's clever
to take your teeth out
and make funny faces.

LINDA GIBSON

When one has reached
eighty-one, one likes
to sit back and let
the world turn by itself,
without trying to push it.

SEAN O'CASEY

If you get tired of replying
to the question,
"To what do you attribute your old age?"
you might answer just as
this old man did,
"The fact that I was born
a very long time ago."

JOHN MYERS

Old age is like a plane flying
through a storm.
Once you're aboard,
there's nothing you can do.
You can't stop the plane,
you can't stop the storm,
you can't stop time.
So one might as well enjoy it.

GOLDA MEIR

Age is full of interest –
wondering which faculty
will desert one next.

CHARLOTTE GRAY

Old friends
disintegrate together –
which enlivens the process.

ODILE DORMEUIL

It's nice to be here.
When you're one hundred years old,
it's nice to be anywhere.

GEORGE BURNS

Old friends help one another
track back through
conversations until they find
what they were originally
talking about.

PAMELA DUGDALE

Never ask old people
how they are if you have
anything else to do that day.

JOE RESTIVO

I am not young enough to know everything.

SIR JAMES M. BARRIE

Your new television will not
come with an instruction manual
because it's so simple it can
be operated by an eight year old –
unfortunately you don't have
an eight year old
to show you how to work it.

STUART & LINDA MACFARLANE

I plan to be an appalling
old woman.
I'm going to boss everyone around.
I'll make people stand up
for me when I come into a room –
and generally capitalize
on all the hypocrisy
that society shows towards the old.

GLENDA JACKSON

Old is not
a state
of mind.
It's a
state
of feet.

PETER GRAY

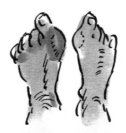

It's essential that you prepare for old age – start the moment you turn eighty.

STUART & LINDA MACFARLANE

If you survive long enough, you're revered – rather like an old building.

KATHARINE HEPBURN

The best part of being an oldie is that you get to be eccentric and young people have to be polite and patronize your idiosyncrasies.

NIELA ELIASON

If beauty is a letter of introduction – wrinkles are a good *résumé*.

MARY ELLEN PICKHAM

How much greater
the pleasure in watching
TV medical dramas
when you've experienced
the plots personally.

PAM BROWN

I have a wonderful
make-up crew.
They're the same people
restoring the Statue of Liberty.

BOB HOPE

The advantage in ageing is being able to have *déjà vu* and amnesia at the same time.

AUTHOR UNKNOWN

I wake up in the middle
of the night knowing
the answer to Life,
the Universe and Everything.
But I've forgotten.

STUART & LINDA MACFARLANE

Refuse to grow old
gracefully. Be as
outrageous as your
weary old frame
will permit.

MATHILDE & SÉBASTIEN FORESTIER

You know you're getting older
when you tell your doctor
that your memory is just fine —
and suddenly your two odd shoes
come into focus.

HELEN THOMSON

I'm so old that...
I don't buy green bananas.
When I order a
three-minute egg at a restaurant,
they ask me for the money up front.
When I travel,
I buy only one-way tickets.

RICHARD LEDERER

I was awestruck this morning
when I discovered that
my wife is some forty years
younger than me.
Sadly I'd just walked into
the wrong house.

BRIAN CLYDE

Senior Moments:
you will remember in vivid detail
a trip to the zoo you had
when you were five
but forget that you put food
in the pot five minutes ago.

STUART & LINDA MACFARLANE

My brother
asked what I'd like
for my 80th birthday.
"To be 40,"
I replied.

LINDA GIBSON

Seventy is not old; at seventy
you are in your prime!
The opposite sex
will find you irresistible.
So slip in your teeth,
dust down your toupee,
polish up your zimmer
and prepare to be hunted.

AMANDA BELL

For a seventy-something
"living life on the edge"
is deciding whether to go to bed
at 8 o'clock or dare
stay up until ten past.

LINDA GIBSON

Age is only
a number –
a very, very big
and frightening
number.

STUART & LINDA MACFARLANE

What I wouldn't give to be seventy again!

OLIVER WENDELL HOLMES JR

The universal motto for the old should be Go Down Fighting.

PAM BROWN

Even now that you are very,
very old you will still be able to do
everything you did as a youth –
it will just take a little longer,
require a bit more effort
and necessitate having a
resuscitation unit on standby.

LINDA GIBSON

Disadvantages of old age...
People giggle at you
when you're on a nudist beach.
When you spot money lying on
the pavement, you can't
bend down to claim it.
You need to take pills to counteract
the side effects of all the other pills.
When you're not in pain
you worry you're dead.
There's no older generation
to blame everything on.

BRIAN CLYDE

At my age,
getting a little action
means your prune
juice is working.

GEORGE BURNS

I like TV better than the movies – it's not so far to the bathroom.

CECIL B. DE MILLE

You'd love to travel still –
if only you could be
issued with a magic carpet
in your living room.

PAM BROWN

At a visit to the surgery
the doctor asked Mary
if she suffered from insomnia.
"I really don't know,"
replied Mary thoughtfully,
"as I need to go to
the bathroom
every fifteen minutes
it's impossible to tell."

STUART & LINDA MACFARLANE

You can get an artificial heart, an artificial kidney, a metal hip socket, a metal elbow joint, a metal kneecap... Today you don't have to worry about getting old, you have to worry about rusting. You don't need a family doctor, just a mechanic who makes house calls. It's great. Every once in a while you have a lube, oil, and tune-up, and instead of an annual physical you get a 10,000-mile check-up. Soon people won't be dying anymore. They'll be traded in.

GEORGE BURNS

I never think of the future. It comes soon enough.

ALBERT EINSTEIN

As I approach a second childhood I endeavour to enter into the pleasures of it.

LADY MARY WORTLEY MONTAGU

They say that once you're
over fifty you start to go into
your second childhood.
I can't wait...
in fact I've made a list of all
the toys I want.

MIKE KNOWLES

Being advanced in years
gives you a wealth of knowledge
and experience to draw on.
Be prepared to pass on your
knowledge by advising doctors,
plumbers, teachers and anyone else
you come into contact with,
how to do their job.

STUART MACFARLANE

"I'm a senior citizen... "
...I'm smiling at you because
I can't hear a word you're saying.
...I'm not grumpy,
I just don't like queues,
traffic,
children,
computers…
...I'm the same as I was
as a teenager –
apart from the wrinkles,
sags and lumps.

STUART & LINDA MACFARLANE

Old age is the only disease you don't look forward to being cured of.

ORSON WELLES

I'm saving that rocking chair for the day when I feel as old as I really am.

DWIGHT D. EISENHOWER

Advantages to attaining old age:
You can sing in the bathroom
while brushing your teeth.
The speed limit is no longer
a challenge to you.
You no longer have to spend big bucks
to get your teeth whitened.
All those things you couldn't have
as a youth you no longer want.
Whatever you buy now won't wear out.
Any sexual harassment charges
filed against you
will probably be dismissed.

JASON LOVE

I have a strict morning routine.
Before I get out of bed
I do a full inventory
of all my ailments:
Do my knees hurt?
Is my gout painful?
Does my back ache?
And so on.
After assessing everything,
if I have got at least three "yeses"
I can be reasonably sure
that I am still alive.

LINDA GIBSON

They tell you that you'll
lose your mind when
you grow older.
What they don't tell you
is that you won't miss
it very much.

MALCOLM COWLEY

I've got to the age
when I need my false teeth
and my hearing aid
before I can ask
where I've left my glasses.

STUART TURNER

E̲verything else
you grow out of but you never
recover from childhood.

BERYL BAINBRIDGE

Experience is what enables you
to make the same mistake
again without getting caught.

RALPH PETERSON

Never buy oldies more
than one bouquet of flowers –
if they wake up surrounded
by flowers
they think they are dead.

MATHILDE & SÉBASTIEN FORESTIER

…you stop lying
about your age
and start
bragging about it.

MARTIN A. RAGAWAY

The heart never becomes wrinkled.

MADAME DE SÉVIGNÉ

It's been so long
since I made love,
I can't remember
who gets tied up!

JOAN RIVERS

I have an obsession for buying fitness videos – though I must admit that the intensity of the exercises I undertake has rapidly decreased in recent years. My latest purchase should be called "Gentle exercises you can do while relaxing on your sofa drinking tea."

AMANDA BELL

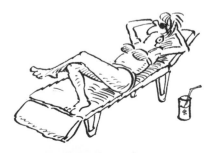

OVER EIGHTIES GLOSSARY

Love:

feelings of affection and lust

you have for chocolate.

Long Term Planning:

Arranging a movie trip

at the weekend.

Sleep:

the most energetic activity

of the day.

Hope:

see Abandon.

Ambition:

a desire to see another sunrise.

Old Age:

A blasphemous expression.

MATHILDE & SÉBASTIEN FORESTIER

If you obey all the rules you miss all the fun.

KATHARINE HEPBURN

The secret of longevity

I can't possibly be 80!
I don't think
I could even count that high
any more.

STUART & LINDA MACFARLANE

I am fed up with looking into mirrors
and seeing my wrinkly old face –
so today I took decisive action.
I printed off some wonderful photos
of my face that were taken
when I was twenty
and have stuck them
on every mirror in the house.

LINDA GIBSON

is to keep breathing.

SOPHIE TUCKER

Eighty is when you can get away
with wearing ridiculous fashion
just like the clothes you wore
when you were eighteen.

BRIAN CLYDE

Like all good ruins, I look better by moonlight.

PHYLLIS DILLER

I'm ninety and still have
my own teeth –
I keep them in a wooden
display box
that I had specially made.

BRIAN CLYDE

How to get your own way:
• Mention the "wound"
whenever asked to do anything.
• Even though you are a
computer whiz kid, act dumb
and let others shop on the internet –
more often than not
they will also end up paying.
• Whenever there's a job
to be done, doze off.

STUART & LINDA MACFARLANE

First you forget names,
then you forget faces,
then you forget
to pull your zipper up,
then you forget to
pull your zipper down.

LEO ROSENBERG

If youth knew;

I downloaded a fantastic App
to help me remember things.
Every twenty minutes
it sends me a reminder
that I downloaded
a fantastic App to help
me remember things.

STUART & LINDA MACFARLANE

if age could.

HENRY ESTIENNE

There comes a point
when all those hilarious
pamphlets offering nose hair
clippers, tip-up armchairs,
walk-in baths and orthopaedic
beds aren't funny any more.

PAM BROWN

You do live longer
with bran, but you
spend the last fifteen years
on the toilet.

ALAN KING

I forget something new every day.

STUART & LINDA MACFARLANE

I love everything about my birthday –
the flowers,
too much to eat,
getting another twenty-two
handkerchiefs...
and, of course,
one can never have
too many pairs of novelty socks!

SÉBASTIEN FORESTIER

Experience is a comb
which nature
gives us
when we are bald.

HELEN VAN SLYKE

Reaching the age of eighty
is like winning
the lottery only to discover
that you have lost the ticket.

STUART & LINDA MACFARLANE

I read that eating
a portion of blueberries
every day will help
to improve memory.
If I can ever remember
to buy some blueberries,
I'll let you know if it works.

LINDA MACFARLANE

There is a sexless bond
that grows up between old men
and women –
based on arthritis and pills.

PAM BROWN

At the age of ninety-five
I married a man thirty years
younger than me. To be honest
I had a long and thorough debate
with myself as to whether marrying
someone so much younger
was a sensible idea.
I was torn in two directions:
My head said, "No"
but my pacemaker said,
"Yes! Yes! Yes!"

STUART & LINDA MACFARLANE

No one is ever old enough to know better.

HOLBROOK JACKSON

My wife threatened to have me replaced by a robot. No chance. Where's she going to find a robot with a dodgy hip and the ability to completely forget everything she ever tells it?

BRIAN CLYDE

Knock Knock.
Who's there?
I am.
I am who?
Now you're getting me confused.

AMANDA BELL

End of Year
Celebration:
Little old me!
Yippeeeee!!!!
I have survived
another year.

STUART & LINDA MACFARLANE